Six Years in Shangrila

Life in a Retirement Complex

by

Victoria Beckett

Drawings by C.J. Schulz

authorHOUSE®

AuthorHouse™
1663 Liberty Drive, Suite 200
Bloomington, IN 47403
www.authorhouse.com
Phone: 1-800-839-8640

First published by AuthorHouse 6/4/2008

ISBN: 978-1-4343-7998-6 (e)
ISBN: 978-1-4343-8002-9 (sc)
Printed in the United States of America
Bloomington, Indiana
Library of Congress Control Number: 2008903466
This book is printed on acid-free paper.

Drawings copyright C.J. Schulz.

Dedication

To a most satisfying life for those who will soon retire

Preface and Acknowledgements

This labor of love shows my wish to share my feelings of good fortune and gratitude for living in such a marvelous facility.

I use the first person perspective to help the reader experience some of the interesting people, helpful staff members, and a host of enjoyable activities. The details are accurate even though actual names of people and places have been changed for anonymity. Jane Schulz, a local artist, adds whimsical drawings, highlighting the main points of each chapter, as well as a delightful cover.

In the past twenty years, an industry of care facilities for the elderly has quietly grown and evolved and is of increasing general interest. This book's primary audience is the 77 million Baby Boomers soon to retire. They need to know what is available so they can choose the best for their own future. Indeed some may now need to find such a facility for their aging parents. Finding an excellent facility is the most practical way to obtain the simplest and happiest lifestyle for one growing older.

I thank all my friends in our retirement home for their friendship and support in good times and bad. I am grateful to the dedicated staff members who meet our many needs. My publisher has given me invaluable aid in producing this book.

Finally, I thank my husband, Dr. Joseph Sharp, for constant encouragement and helpful editing. Needless to say, all errors are mine, but I hope they will be forgiven if this book proves rewarding to my readers.

CONTENTS

"Welcome, I am Eleanor, of the Welcome Committee

Chapter 1: To Shangrila

I moved into Shangrila, a retirement complex, expecting only a comfortable place to live in, and found a wonderful, heart-warming environment to spend the rest of my days.

First, here is a thumbnail summary. Three hundred independent apartment residents form a close community of people who share companionship and support each other in times of trouble. I've made a number of new friends here. The food is simply marvelous. I love having my apartment cleaned every week, and my plumbing, electricity, heating, and other problems immediately repaired at no extra expense. I am comforted by quick access to excellent medical care. There is a top-notch exercise program, and I have been encouraged to teach a weekly tai chi class. The many daily activities here include concerts, presented talks, and shopping tours. In essence,

I'm enjoying a hassle-free life full of entertaining and intellectual activities. Every year the chief administrator reports on the past year's good annual results. I am thrilled to belong to this active, caring community.

Who would have thought the Y2K computer crisis would catapult John and me into a whole new life? We weren't seeking an elegant start to the twenty-first century, just a way to avoid freezing in my Minnesota house in January. Because the vital computers that manage power and fuel hadn't been properly programmed to recognize the new century, our utilities might cut off on January 1, 2000. In the last few years, computer programmers all over the world frantically revised millions of computer instructions, but there was no guarantee they could finish in time. Since our house ran on gas and electricity and had neither a fireplace nor an oil burner, we might well be left to cope with freezing temperatures.

I always try to anticipate problems, so when I couldn't find a solution to this threat, I enlisted my husband's help.

"What shall we do, John?" I asked him. He leaned back in his chair to think about it with his usual amused look. He is a white-haired, laid-back computer scientist with a round head, slightly lined face, high forehead, pink skin, and hazel-blue eyes that peer through silver-rimmed glasses—a lovely man who holds all my affections.

He could not assure me our utility company could keep our house warm, so he finally replied, "Well, my dear, I can think of only two solutions. We could stay with your elderly friend with the oil-burning stove until the crisis is over. On the other hand, didn't you tell me we are already down on the waiting list for Shangrila retirement home? Of course, if we decide to move there it would be permanent. Are you ready for this?

My friend, Mrs. B, replied, "Sure, you and John are welcome to come here, but it would be crowded. You'll have to sleep in your sleeping bags on the floor."

The retirement home marketing manager happily answered, "You are in luck. We just had a cancellation, so we can take you in January."

We were going to move there eventually, so why not now? John didn't think we were ready for a retirement place, but it was an attractive solution to our dilemma.

≈

At Shangrila, we chose a two-bedroom apartment that faced south for good fung shui (good fortune). There were two bathrooms and corridors wide enough to pass a wheelchair through; they proved very handy. The living room, kitchen, and walk-in closet were adequate. After we measured the rooms, John drew a plan outlining where our furniture would be placed. With Shangrila's help, we added new carpeting, fluorescent lighting, and a tall bookcase to stand along the entire front corridor. For his computers and their special wiring, John arranged a center table in the largest bedroom, which was to be his study.

Nothing prepared us for the difficult move. Twenty years of accumulated clutter had to be ruthlessly pruned. It was agonizing to pick what to take and what to discard. Clothes, books, furniture, china, documents, and papers; these things held deep memories. Squeezing our four-bedroom house into a two-bedroom apartment has been a monumental task. In fact, even years later, we are still discarding things.

I packed the essentials, and then piled the rest in the front living-dining room for disposal. For more than a month, things were sold; given away, hauled away to rummage sales, the Salvation Army, Goodwill, or finally tossed into the county dump. On an icy morning with a trace of snow on the ground, movers carted our things to our new apartment. Enjoying the warm 72-degree temperature inside our apartment, we knew we had solved our heat problem. We discovered later that moving in early has advantages. The older one becomes, the more daunting the process.

Ironically, the Y2K problem was smoothly solved on time, without jeopardizing our institutions.

❧

We had barely arrived at our apartment when a housekeeper arrived to help me unpack kitchenware from the boxes all over the floor into the kitchen shelves. Soon a kindly welcome-committee lady, in a comfortable sweater and slacks, knocked and entered.

"Welcome," she said with a big smile. "My name is Eleanor. I will introduce you to Shangrila. Ask me any questions. Here, start with these." She pressed a fragrant loaf of raisin bread into my hands. Then she handed me a slim booklet, *Shangrila Resident Handbook*; several stapled sheets comprising the *Staff and Resident Phone Directory*, and the *Weekly Update* that announced weekly events. I hoped there were not many rules and regulations.

"I know you are busy, so I won't stay, but I'd like to show you the trash closet and the laundry room on this floor before I leave. You will be using these places a great deal. At five thirty p.m. I'll come to take you both to supper."

She returned promptly at five thirty and took us up to the dining room at the top of this high-rise building. John and I were astonished to look through a row of continuous windows to see a spectacular view of familiar buildings below. The sensation was like being on top of a rotating tower, except this place was stationary. As we watched the sun begin to set, the reddish blue sky slowly darkened and a few lights flickered on here and there.

We checked in at the dinner reception desk and were shown to a table for four with snowy white tablecloth and napkins, and sparkling silverware. The service by a cheerful, young waitress was excellent, and the food we chose from a large menu was delicious. We could hardly believe such a first-class meal would be our daily fare.

Throughout the meal, Eleanor continuously chatted with us about the contents of the handbook. After supper, she took us down to the first-floor lobby and introduced us to the receptionist, who is the pivotal person to call with any questions or services requests. On the counter was a sign-up book for upcoming bus trips to more remote concerts, excursions, shopping tours, and other fun activities. To her left was a wall of message slots for newspapers and internal notices, and still farther left were rows of locked individual mailboxes.

Continuing to the south side of the building, we entered a well-stocked library. The latest books were in a middle bookcase and older books lined the walls. At one end were the card index drawers. Eleanor showed us how to find a book by author or title. On another shelf were several daily newspapers. A person sat in a chair nearby, reading a paper, while another dozed. I knew I would be back often.

Finally, she took us to the fifth-floor exercise room to see two bright new treadmill machines, two exercise bicycles, and two TV consoles. Next-door was an open exercise room. As we bid Eleanor goodnight, we thanked her for her lovely welcome.

In the following days, I studied the handbook to learn more about this amazing place.

Each resident automatically receives twenty-six paid lunches or dinners per month, and a weekly housekeeper to clean the apartment. We also had access to maintenance service for hanging pictures, clearing clogged drains, fixing thermometers, and other chores and maintenance. Twice yearly, they also check the fire alarms and clean the window and screens. There is also a separate beauty parlor and a small shop on the lobby floor for grocery items.

Shangrila is called a retirement complex because it offers a continuum of care. In addition to the independent-living apartments like ours, there are forty-five assisted-living rooms for the more disabled and about thirty supportive-care rooms for the severely disabled (like rooms in nursing homes). A seamless transition can be made from one to another if the need arises. There is a short-stay skilled-care unit of thirty beds used by the adjacent medical center for discharged patients who still need intensive physical therapy and occupational therapy before returning home.

On the third floor is a health center consisting of a few nurses who can come to your apartment to provide various health needs or send you to the hospital when necessary. Every problem seems to have been anticipated.

We have a skyway for convenient indoor access to the nearby medical center and downtown areas. By way of tunnel or skyway, we have access to most of downtown, including shopping malls, banks, restaurants, bookstores, the public library, civic auditorium, and government buildings.

This means that in Minnesota winters we can do many errands without ever going outdoors. Furthermore, Shangrila has a seventeen-seat van that stops daily at more remote clinics, supermarkets, and shopping sites. Residents who no longer drive use this extensively. John and I still keep our car in the basement garage but hardly use it anymore. He likes to joke that "We fill our car with gas every month, whether it needs it or not."

Soon after our arrival, we met Barbara the very important activities coordinator. Indeed very few activities happen without her cheerful, effective leadership. She is about five-foot-six and has a round face framed by reddish straight hair. She is bouncing with energy. Our activities coordinator has become our first and last resource. She schedules one-to-two-day trips to nearby cities. We visit the Guthrie Theater, sculptured gardens, arboretum, museum of art, Mall of America shopping center, Mississippi River Cruises, Apple Orchard Center, Upper Minnesota-Duluth City, and more, always stopping for great food. Barbara usually joins in herself to guarantee an enjoyable trip.

She also schedules events inside Shangrila: concerts (adults or children singing or playing instruments), talks (by county officers, police, doctors, lawyers, or businessmen on a variety of pertinent subjects), and weekend movies, as well as holiday celebrations for New Year's, Easter, the Fourth of July, Halloween, and Christmas. Once a month she invites women speakers to the women's luncheon. The men schedule their own speakers for their monthly men's breakfast. Such a plethora of activities ensures no one is left out or bored. Good attendance attests to the residents' enthusiasm.

All activities are described in a weekly bulletin. Since there are often too many to keep in mind, Barbara posts large, colorful, illustrated daily posters in the elevators. My husband says, with a laugh, that they are more useful than the weekly bulletin.

Once a year Barbara organizes an enormous sidewalk sale. All residents donate discards and wholeheartedly help in sorting, pricing, and selling piles of goods. Huge crowds line up hours ahead of time to be the first inside for this major event. The thousands of dollars earned are donated to local charities, so everyone gains in this win-win activity.

We have indeed become members of a well-organized little community.

Watering his Plant Cart - "Enjoy."

Chapter 2: Friends and Acquaintances

Who comes to Shangrila? The average age of a resident newcomer is seventy-five, but the overall average age of those living here is eighty-five. The most common profession is teaching, both among men and women. Since we are near a medical center, there are also quite a few retired physicians and nurses. Retired businessmen are the next largest group. Among us are also a few photographers, painters, and musicians. The ratio here is about three women to two men. Most residents are Caucasians from the Midwest, but a few come from other states on both the east and west coasts. Some are foreign-born but became U.S. citizens. Many originally came for medical care at the nearby medical center, and then decided to stay close by to continue their care. Often couples come when one is ill or disabled. Widows and widowers come because they don't want to live alone or wish to stop caring for their house. Alternatively, a few residents live in Shangrila but maintain a house outside for short-term stays.

~

Here are a few stories of people I have come to know, both as friends and acquaintances. They particularly stand out in my mind.

Lucy was one hundred years old this spring. Until two years ago, she drove her own car around town. In addition, although she now uses a walker, her white hair is tastefully curled, her clothes are pretty and colorful, and she always wears a beautiful smile. She takes part in exercise classes and goes in the van on short town trips and to concerts and lectures. Her quiet opinions are still so interesting she is a joy to be around. I hope to be like her at a hundred.

Jerry was in her late eighties when she contacted me soon after my arrival and asked me (but not my husband) to tea in her apartment. Before retirement, she had been in charge of United Nations nurses and health education in the third world, from Africa to the Middle East, to Asia. Her manner was a cross between that of a civil servant and a nurse. Her apartment was full of beautiful Asian furniture and treasures. She was petite, trim, and well dressed, often in lovely silks. "Look at this tapestry," she would say. "It was given to me as a token of thanks from the Afghan government. I taught some Muslim women nurses who had to be covered from head to foot. I could recognize them only by their feet." An artificial fireplace made her place warm and cozy even when we could see snow through the windows. She was alone, without relatives, and she carefully selected those she invited to tea. Since she passed away, I have missed her exotic presence.

Blanche was in her nineties, somewhat gaunt, plainly dressed, and she wore glasses at the tip of her nose. In our dining committee meetings, she always asked for the "plain food" she had been used to. When someone commented that was old-fashioned, she retorted, "But I'm not old." A former teacher, she was used to having young people around. She maintained her youthful spirit by sponsoring a group of Asian medical students and residents in training from the nearby medical center. She often filled a table full of these young people for meals in the dining room. She listened to their worries and triumphs, and loaned them money when they were short. In return, they helped her buy and set up a small computer and taught her how to use e-mail; they brought her books to read and music disks to play. After some years, she became feeble and knew her time had come. She feared dying alone but refused to burden her young people with her illness. One found out about her condition and quickly contacted the others. For more than a week, a rotating group stayed at her bedside day and night. When Blanche finally drew her last breath, she was surrounded by the young people who loved her and had been a joy in her life.

Ulysses was a Greek businessman rumored to be quite wealthy. He had lived in Shangrila many years, and everyone knew him. Well into his nineties, he was a small, dapper, bespectacled man with scanty gray hair and mustache, who greeted all comers with a friendly "Hi, how are you?" Every year he gave himself a huge birthday party and invited the whole retirement home as well as all his Greek friends. He would wear his best suit and, teetering on his cane, greet each guest with obvious enjoyment. The food was always sumptuous. The Father of the Greek Orthodox Church would first say a prayer, and then we would all heartily sing "Happy Birthday." Every spring he would sell tickets to the Greek Festival to raise money for his church. At his urging, many of us went to enjoy the Greek food and dancing. He was one of a kind; we miss him.

Kari lived here with her 102-year-old Danish mother. She had been a home economics professor; a great cook and home decorator, but most of all, she was a devoted daughter. I remember the birthday parties she gave for her mother. She invited all the residents to enjoy special

Danish treats. Her mother sat in a wheelchair, graciously accepting everyone's best wishes. When her mother died, Kari returned to live in her condo, near her friends and colleagues. She had stayed in Shangrila only to care for her mother.

An early resident, Carl, a former college president, now nearing ninety, contributes significantly to our entertainment. Every weekend he shares famous old movies from his enormous collection. The Charlie Chaplin movies are my favorites. On Thursdays he shares videos of famous big band and orchestra music dating from the '40s to '90s. Both events draw sizeable crowds who enjoy remembering those "good old days."

Louis, although bent forward on his walker and also nearing ninety, is one of the founders of our Green Thumb plant room, where he still grows orchids. I often see him watering his beloved flowers with a small watering can. The room is now full of varied beautiful plants belonging to different owners who find this an ideal nursery because of its fluorescent light, high humidity, steady warm temperature, and good upkeep. For the enjoyment of those who walk by the second-floor skyway, Louis has placed there a large plant cart with a shining overhead fluorescent light. He has filled it with varied green succulent plants with tiny pink or yellow flowers. I always stop by to look and feel refreshed.

My special friend, Janice, well into her nineties, had been a noted obstetrician. She was a pioneer for legal abortion. Tall and thin, she was always beautifully dressed, her hair tastefully coifed and regal in demeanor. She had been quite a controversial figure. In fact, many had wanted her jailed, while others thought her a champion. Roe vs. Wade finally vindicated her work. Her many grateful patients remember her well. When we came to know her at Shangrila, we discovered the steel hand in her velvet glove, the staunch champion of women's causes. I often visited her to talk about her past, which would have made a fascinating book. Before her death she told me she had boxes of voluminous notes on her life's work. Perhaps someone will still write it up. A great lady, she should not be forgotten.

I have often wondered how the many devoted spouses of the impaired could be so patient, so gentle. Perhaps it is not so hard when you love someone dearly and remember how they once were. Marjorie is a tiny, strong woman. Frequently I saw her pushing hard to propel a wheelchair holding her heavy husband. His mind became unclear after a cerebral hemorrhage. Ironically, he had been an authority on this condition. She faithfully pushed him to many medical meetings where his colleagues greeted him with fondness.

Nancy's husband had brain surgery and could no longer care for himself. She provides all his care with cheerful grace. She sometimes leaves him in the care of the assisted living unit to get time off to shop and perhaps go to a movie. I salute her; few women can manage so well.

Allen pushed his wife in a wheelchair for more than a year as she progressively drooped, until she finally was no longer aware of her surroundings. Sitting next to her quiet form, he would often talk of their previous happy life together and of her unusual craft skills. His gentle caring never wavered. Since her death, he still gives parties to remember and celebrate her life. A deep love indeed.

Jason has a different way. His wife had a stroke and is mostly wheelchair bound, except that with help she can stand and walk a short distance. She is always comfortably and neatly dressed but says very little. He is an extremely active man of faith, performing helpful activities around Shangrila and participating in many committees. He simply brings her along to quietly watch and listen. They seem as comfortable with this arrangement as we all are.

Our constant pleasant interaction is the unique quality of living here. We meet each other in the hallways, in the elevators, at meals, in the eatery, in exercise classes, on trips, and at the concerts and seminars. We visit sick friends in their apartments or in the hospital; one woman brings communion to bedridden Catholics. I know residents who take their friends for treatments at the medical center; others buy groceries for their friends. We are also in constant friendly interaction with our cleaning lady, maintenance staff, waitresses, receptionist, and hairdresser. John and I feel that these many social contacts, as well as access to good medical care and hassle-free living, seem to extend people's lives and make them happier. We hope it will do the same for us.

We notice that residents who move in early, before age has taken its toll, seem to do best. They have the interest and energy to participate in the array of activities. Of course, the decision to move is hard, but we have found it worthwhile. We found the expense of living here no more than that of living in our house. One resident in her eighties said, "My biggest regret is not coming in ten years ago."

Friends have always been a vital part of my life, especially during a long widowhood, after my first husband's death. My life would have been lonely had I not shared rich and varied experiences with many friends. I arrived at Shangrila to find old friends and coworkers. From this nucleus, I soon made many new friends. As older friends passed on, younger vibrant arrivals become friends: a continuous renewal that makes this a blessed place to live in.

Death is no stranger here; it gradually ceases to be feared and almost becomes a friend. When our time comes, we expect to gently enter another sphere, to join loved ones who have gone before.

Tai chi class - "Now, cross hands."

Chapter 3: Engagement

I believe that to really know a place, one has to play an active part in the community. There are a number of committees for residents to join. As a natural joiner, I jumped in feet first. Because I love cooking and food, I first joined the dining committee. About a dozen of us sat around a table once a month with the dietitian menu writer, the chief cook, and the dining room director. We reviewed resident complaints and suggestions. I soon realized it was impossible to satisfy everyone! Some liked the plates hotter; some said they burnt their hands. Some wanted smaller helpings; others wanted them larger. Some wanted no salt on the food; others wanted it well seasoned. Some wanted innovative entrees; others wanted plain dishes. The accommodating staff helped us compromise.

I began to understand how complex food management is. After food is bought in bulk, its sanitation and safety are paramount. For example, when spinach was reported contaminated with E. coli bacteria in California, no spinach was served until it was safe again. At the end of the year, the whole committee walked through the kitchen to observe with surprised delight the scope of the well-organized enterprise.

Food encompasses much more than just the daily dining room meal. On Sundays and holidays, we have a delicious midday buffet of many varieties of salads; entrees of beef, pork, chicken, fish; tasty potatoes and vegetables; and a choice of several desserts. These are wonderful occasions to invite relatives or friends.

Sometimes we residents prefer phoning ahead to order a take-out meal from the weekly menu. The food items are packed in plastic containers and placed in a large plastic bag to be picked up by us at the time requested. The hot dishes stay hot. We can then enjoy our meal in our apartment while watching television.

Two years ago, Shangrila started offering a separate buffet three evenings a week featuring regional or ethnic foods. It is held in a smaller dining room next to the main one, which also has a great view. Dress is casual. John and I went the night that featured a Pacific Northwest menu. The buffet table had Pike Place Market salad, seafood stew, corn and zucchini medley, sour dough bread, and Oregon blueberry cake. Drinks were a choice of wine, punch, coffee, and tea. After filling our plate, we sat down with friends at a table for six persons and enjoyed a delicious meal while chatting with friends.

The top floor has another medium size dining room with a lovely view. It is reserved for catered parties. John gave me a surprise birthday party there. My neighbor pretended a mutual friend wanted me to join her for supper upstairs. On arrival, picture my astonishment to find a long table covered with food and surrounded by twelve smiling friends and John. Then they all sang "Happy Birthday" with gusto.

The room is also perfect for celebrating wedding anniversaries and family reunions. John and I have had fun attending several of these. Another room function is a fortnightly, Friday "wine and cheese" affair. Volunteers act as hosts; John and I hosted one. The appetizers and drinks are on a table at the end of the room, and incoming people help themselves, and then sit down at various small tables. The hosts go around topping up their drinks while everyone chats with each other. People come and go, usually going on to supper in the main dining room. Unfortunately, all these eating pleasures entice us to gain weight, which we must later try to lose.

During our first year, I gave a demonstration of Chinese cooking. I borrowed a large electric wok and brought my own electric rice cooker. I put equal amounts of white and brown rice into my rice cooker and let it cook away while I stir-fried first the pineapple with chicken then the asparagus with carrots in sesame oil in the wok. Within half an hour, the audience sampled this delicious meal. Afterward I handed out printed recipes. I think older people should try stir-fry cooking because it is simple, low calorie, and offers a wide variety of appetizing recipes.

Tai chi exercises are particularly suitable for the elderly, since it is slow moving, easy to do, and teaches good balance. Since I had been teaching tai chi and yoga classes in the local health club, I easily obtained permission to start a modified tai chi exercise class at Shangrila. I eliminated the harder yoga poses and floor exercises so students wouldn't have to struggle to get up. Later I added some Feldenkrais and Pilates movements. I started in an open area on the roof but later moved the class indoors to the carpeted fitness exercise room on the fifth floor, where it is still held every Tuesday morning. The popular class has earned me the title of tai chi teacher.

Later a full-time fitness coordinator, Laura, was hired. To our surprise, in a few months this pretty brown-eyed young woman cajoled almost half the residents into either taking an exercise class or using the exercise machines. She started first by assessing our abilities, then placing us in one of three groups: those moderately disabled (on canes and walkers), those of average mobility, and those who are very mobile. Then she devised daily exercise classes suitable for each group. I was pleased to receive her support for my tai chi class. It was a particular joy to see some exercise participants who had had a stroke or orthopedic surgery improve from walker to cane and some to full mobility. For men (who seem to prefer machines to classes), she added several new weight-pressing machines to a bigger machine room. All our activities attendances are recorded. Every three months our fitness is reassessed so she can prepare individual reports listing both previous and current performance. Most of us are pleased by measured improvement, encouraging us to do more.

In addition, on nice summer and fall days, Laura schedules trail walks through the local parks twice weekly. I remember my first time out on a sparkling sunny day in June. The van dropped us at a nearby park. We walked on a leveled dirt road, fringed on both sides with trees, along a flowing stream. Birds were singing and an occasional bee buzzed by. We walked at our own speed for about twenty minutes and walked twenty minutes back. Then we met the van and returned to Shangrila. What a treat! This splendid teacher encouraged us to increase our mobility by getting regular exercise at an age when one expects decreasing mobility.

Not all my ideas bore fruit. The saddest part of living in Shangrila is the death of a spouse, which devastates the surviving spouse. I wanted to use my support group experience to help bereaved spouses work out their feelings among others similarly bereaved spouses. With Shangrila's permission, I started such a group. I stressed three cardinal rules: no interruption, no advice, and strict confidentiality. Success depended on strict adherence. Unfortunately, a participant could not keep silent. Perhaps it is inevitable in such a close community. As soon as a cardinal rule was violated, the group had to be disbanded. Many felt this was a great loss.

Next, I joined the quite large library committee. Most of us were asked to spend one hour a week as the library desk attendant. During this often-busy hour, we checked in returned books, placed books back on the shelves, tidied the newspapers, and helped residents find books. One came to know where to quickly find books. At times, we would also work in pairs to label new books. A selection subcommittee suggests new books to buy and chooses which to keep among many donated books. Periodically books that are seldom read are weeded out so the total number of books remains constant. I soon learned who the hardest working committee members were. I also discovered that the most popular books are mysteries. Next are biographies, and romances are third. Although many residents have a professional background, I was surprised that the least popular books were those on political or scientific subjects.

At the end of my second year on the committee, we began the arduous task of going electronic. The entire contents of the library had to be computerized. Out went the old Dewey card index. After about two years, we completed a nicely working system. Great credit goes to the committee members who spent many hours to accomplish this. Never say an old dog can't learn new tricks. Our heavily used, first-class library contributes greatly to the joy of living here.

An important committee that I haven't joined is the arts and decorating committee. Harry is a one-time prominent lawyer, now in his nineties. He's partly blind and deaf but is still clear-headed. Harry entered Shangrila many years ago with his wife. When she died, he donated their entire collection of hundreds of copies of famous paintings to Shangrila in her name. They came from renowned museums such as the Boston Museum of Fine Arts. The arts committee has cataloged then distributed them to every corridor. Harry's donation was such a magnificent, generous gift, and what luck we had this group to take charge. The committee also exhibits residents' art objects in an enclosed display cabinet in the lobby. They include beautiful art made of wood, stone, metal, cotton, or porcelain. Finally, the committee maintains fresh floral bouquets in frequently used spots in the lobby. All this surrounding beauty is wonderfully uplifting.

I soon met the spiritual coordinator, or chaplain named Martha. She is a small, dignified woman who stands very straight and has a clear voice that carries well in services. She holds ecumenical vespers every Sunday afternoon in our lovely little chapel with its stained-glass window, organ, piano, alter, and pulpit. Her straightforward fifteen-minute sermons usually contain one or two points that can easily be remembered. She also holds a weekly Bible study class. Lately she has offered a Wednesday "Faith in Today's World" class to open our eyes to today's religious beliefs. When I was in the hospital, her short visits and simple prayers were a real comfort. During the week she is in and out of her lobby floor office and is available by phone anytime we need her.

One day, much troubled by my sister-in-law's death from cancer, I asked her, "Where is she? Is she in the Christian heaven of angels and harps? Or is her spirit roaming the galaxy and right now perched on my shoulder? Is she born again in another form, as the Buddhists believe? Or is death the end, and all is extinguished and there is nothing, a blank?" Of course, there are no proven answers, but it was a relief to discuss my ideas with her.

She also conducts memorial services in our chapel for residents who have passed away. This gives us an opportunity to say goodbye to friends whom we have enjoyed and will miss.

~

After living here a year, I was elected to the residents' council, an august group of residents who are a liaison between the residents and the administration. Each month we heard reports from each committee. Then we discussed and recommended the best ideas to the administration. One such suggestion was proposed by Mary, a physician who returned to Minnesota after practicing in a city in the northeast. Soon after her arrival, she noticed the run-down condition of the nearby little park. The city mowed the grass periodically but took no other responsibility for it. The grass and walks were often littered with cigarette butts and old papers. Her proposal to the council was:

"I want to organize a group of volunteers to clean the park with rakes once a month. We could do this from spring to fall. It would provide a good outdoor workout, and we would end up with a clean and pleasant place to walk, sit or picnic."

The council enthusiastically approved the project. She and Barbara, the activities coordinator, designed the project together. They organized teams to paint brightly colored large disposal cans to hold cigarettes and papers. These cans were then distributed around the park. On designated days, volunteers were provided with rakes and gloves to clean up the park. We were delighted to see users begin putting their trash in the new cans. The park has become a very attractive place exactly as Mary envisioned.

The council work gave me an overall picture of how the whole system functions. It helped me appreciate the administration's concern that the residents have adequate input and understand how practical and helpful ideas are acted upon.

We now have added June, our new computer coordinator, who oversees the computer uses of various Shangrila facilities. She also holds fortnightly meetings to teach residents how to use the computer. She is available to assist individuals with their computer problems. There are public computers for residents' use on the third floor and in the library. A few of us are slowly becoming adept at their use.

Residents also initiate their own groups to meet regularly. There are bridge groups, Scrabble groups, singing groups, billiards groups, photography groups, golfing groups, and more. If one cannot find a group of interest, one can start a group if enough people will join.

Various residents have given evening seminars on subjects about which they are knowledgeable. My husband John is one such contributor. Full of ideas and a gifted teacher, he likes to study new topics in detail, and then teach what he has learned. Over the years, he has presented talks on Genomics, Muslim history, investing, computer systems, Tivo TV devices, and human anatomy to name a few. He illustrates these talks with slides and DVDs. The good attendance and intelligent questions show appreciation of his efforts that add to the Shangrila experience.

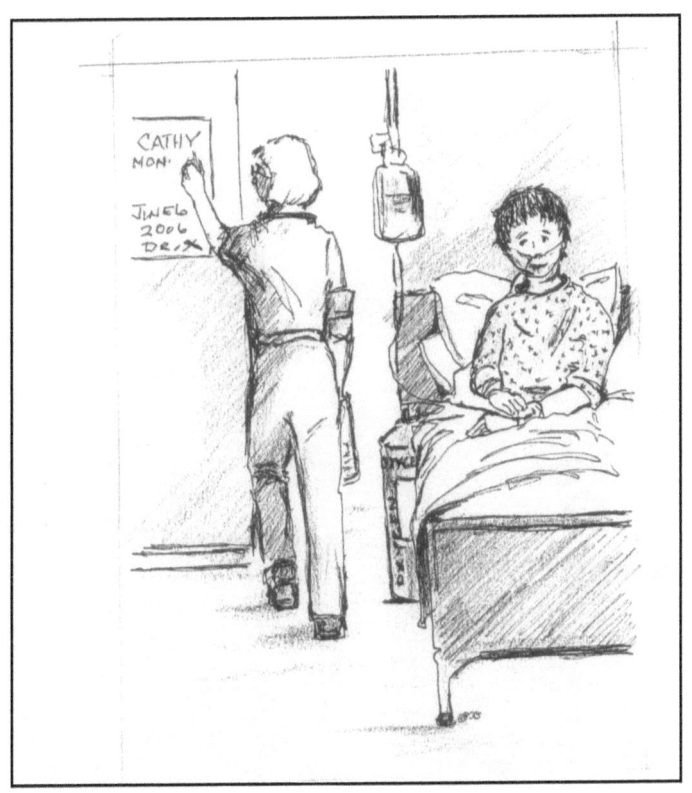

Hospital nurse writes on white board

CHAPTER 4: Illness Onslaught

The waning June sunlight glowed through the large west window, lighting a strange white room where I lay on a hospital bed. At last, all was finally quiet. Turning my head slightly, I could see a row of blinking lights behind me, and looking forward, I saw "Cathy, Monday, June 6, 2002, Dr. X." written on a small white board.

I had just lived through a busy hospital day, constantly interrupted by questions and tests. The present quiet would be short-lived, but I had a moment to think back on how I got here.

About six o'clock this morning, I awoke feeling like I was burning up. As I groped to the bathroom, my legs almost buckled.

I called out, "John, I feel terrible. Something is very wrong." He bundled me into our car and rushed me to the nearby emergency room. Since I had been blessed with good health all my life, I was stunned to suddenly feel so sick. As weak and miserable as I felt, a part of me watched with fascination at all the changes in medical practice that occurred during the ten years I've been retired.

At the emergency room, the doctors immediately scanned my electronic medical record, quickly asked a few questions, and gave me a brief physical exam. Meanwhile, a young nurse gently removed my clothes, got me into a hospital gown, and recorded my vital signs (Temperature – high 102, pulse – fast 90, blood pressure - below normal 83/40, blood oxygen saturation - below normal 88). Another nurse drew blood for lab tests, then carefully threaded and firmly taped a needle into my forearm vein. This needle was connected to a plastic line that in turn led to a plastic bag of intravenous fluid hanging on a nearby stand. She then attached two plastic bracelets to my wrist. One was bar-coded with my name, date of birth, and clinic number, to be carefully checked before every procedure. The second indicated I wanted to be resuscitated if my heart stopped. Next, she added life-saving antibiotics and other medicines into the intravenous fluid. Finally, she inserted a small plastic tube into each nostril that was connected to a nearby oxygen tank. I soon felt the cool oxygen flowing into my nose and throat. After consultation, the doctors decided to hospitalize me.

Arriving at my hospital room on a four-wheeled bed cart, I was introduced to a young doctor and several nurses. After a more leisurely series of questions and physical exams, they restarted tracking my vital signs. Later in the afternoon, the senior staff physician, Dr. X, entered with a retinue of young doctors. After more questions, he examined my heart, lungs, and abdomen, then explained his assessment and plan of action.

"We think you have active and uncontrolled autoimmune hemolytic anemia (my immune system was mistakenly destroying my own red cells)." I recalled a mild anemia had shown up several months ago. He continued, "We will obtain additional laboratory tests to confirm this and try to discover what triggered this sudden red cell drop. It is often caused by a treatable infection." He then outlined the next few days' treatment: IV fluids (graduated to liquid diet after a day), blood transfusions, antibiotics, cortisone, pain medication as needed, bathroom privileges (with help), and daily walks (with help).

Surprisingly teams of specialized nurses and technicians carried out my tests instead of the single multitasked nurse of my day. Each specialist performed one specific task. One drew blood; another gave blood.

One checked bladder capacity; another took portable x-rays. One took portable electrocardiograms; another measured echocardiograms. One handled cultures; another handled tissue biopsies. They repeated the same task over and over on different patients, on different floors. There was no fumbling or hesitation when they worked on me.

A head nurse presided at the center station. A practical nurse was assigned to me for the day, who in turn supervised several nurse aids. My doctors, internists and hematologists, seemed absurdly young but were courteous, kind, and patient, and their alert intelligence gave me confidence in their judgment. I felt I was getting first-class medical care and also realized such a labor-intensive hospital stay must be expensive.

Every day a practical nurse wrote her first name, the day of the week, the date, and my doctor's name on my white board. This small courtesy helped me stay oriented during the hectic hospital days.

The nurses were marvelous. I always believed nurses were the patients' salvation, since they actually carried out the orders and did the "laying of hands." They were never cross or brusque, even when I was irritable and they were tired. When I punched the call button, they came in quickly, cheerfully did their job, and left. For the first time, I also had pleasant and efficient nurses who were male, Hispanic, or Asian.

Another surprise was the new, more precise technology. My temperature was not taken with a mercury-tipped stick thermometer placed under my tongue but rather by a plastic earpiece, with a digital read-out, briefly inserted in one ear. My blood pressure was not taken by listening with a stethoscope but rather by an arm cuff that automatically inflates and deflates while recording a digital read-out on the wall panel. Blood oxygen saturation was measured by a clothespin-like gadget clipped to my index finger. New, more accurate equipment supplanted what I was used to.

A small stand-up monitor that automatically controlled the flow of IV fluids into my arm intrigued me. A small panel flashed a message to the center station when the fluid was blocked or needed a refill. Each warning was announced by a gentle *beep, beep*, which continued until the attending nurse fixed the problem and turned the alarm off. This remarkable device anticipates problems and contributes to patient safety.

The first few days and nights in the hospital saw a continuous flow of people and activities. Each hour, around the clock, a nurse, doctor, or technician would come for some specific task. Either someone was asking me questions, answering my queries, collecting blood, or wheeling me to another room for a procedure. Needle sticks were painful, especially because there were many. A stream of technicians took sample cultures from numerous orifices to try to locate a possible infection. I was exhausted and longed for a few hours of uninterrupted rest or sleep.

Full of dread, I anxiously began to ponder life and death. I frequently heard urgent "code" intercom calls and saw doctors and nurses rush to nearby beds, presumably in desperate efforts to save someone's life. What would happen if I became incapacitated? What final words did I wish to leave my loved ones? Were my important papers clear and easy to locate? Were my will and estate plans up to date? Such gloomy thoughts went 'round and round' in my head. Intermittently I was angry, asking myself, "Why me?" and thinking, "This isn't fair!" Between steeling myself against painful intrusions and dwelling on my possible death, I was a miserable wreck.

As I gradually responded to treatment and gathered strength, my spirits rallied. I started to take food and medicines by mouth, and the staff began removing my tubes. Slowly my vital signs became normal, my abnormal laboratory tests improved, and to everyone's relief, no new abnormalities appeared. My doctors began to plan my transfer for temporary rehabilitation at the Shangrila skilled care unit. One of the young doctors explained the significance of all my laboratory reports and how I was to conduct myself after discharge. I was given a computer printout of my hospital stay, discharge instructions, and new prescriptions. My ever-supportive husband happily made plans to take me home. The sun was finally coming out from behind the clouds. I had hope again. How wonderful to rejoin the living!

I dwell in detail about my hospitalization because it is a common painful experience of almost all Shangrila residents. We "grin and bear it", hoping it will not be repeated, and thankful for the fine recovery facilities at Shangrila. I learned I owed my life to medical, technical advances and the caring, competent hospital staff. We residents must have easy access to prompt, necessary medical care because body parts break down as we age. Alas, this was just the beginning of six years of hospitalizations and surgeries. Two surgeries assisted in controlling my anemia, two removed benign tumors, and two repaired a hip fracture. Much as I dreaded each necessary hospitalization, I was glad no malignancies were found and was grateful for each good recovery. John said I am pretty tough. I resolved to seek physical resilience by a balance of diet, exercise, and rest. I would seek emotional and spiritual equanimity through prayer and meditation.

I grew much closer to my dear husband, who actually slept in my hospital room many nights when I felt battered and bruised. He encouraged me in every step of my recovery. In my absences, he learned to do the laundry, clean up, and buy groceries. When I returned to the apartment, he helped me in and out of bed, put on pressure stockings, and walked with me as I used a cane or walker. We realized how dependent we were on each other, physically and emotionally. I am lucky to have a good man at my side.

Each hospitalization brought an avalanche of get-well cards and flowers from Shangrila friends who cheered me up and made me feel remembered. I greatly appreciate their thoughtful concern.

After my hip fracture, my husband and members of the facility's maintenance service made our apartment safer to prevent another fall. First, all small throw rugs were removed. Wall-to-wall carpeting was installed in both the kitchen and my bathroom. (I had fallen on the hard kitchen floor.) A wooden floorboard was placed under a swivel chair next to my desk to allow easy movement between the desk and file cabinets. A curtain replaced the closet door so we could move the bed sideways to make more room at the desk. In my bathroom, the tub was replaced with a walk-in shower with many hand bars added on the wall. A higher toilet seat was installed. We try to leave nothing on the floor that one might slip on. I now feel completely safe in the apartment. I believe these changes will protect us both as we become older and less steady.

Two things kept me going during these stressful years: my tai chi class and writing a book. I desperately wanted to continue the tai chi class, both to benefit the participants and myself. The thought of returning to my class (which blessed substitutes had kept going) encouraged me to vigorously exercise after each surgery.

The book was another important interest. I had started it several years ago in a desultory manner during some creative writing classes at the local community college. There is an old saying that the best way to combat woes is to concentrate on something else. So I thought, why not take my mind off my health by writing a book?

This was a grand new venture. I learned the ups and downs of publishing and marketing. Nevertheless, I eagerly returned to writing after each hospital stay. I found it fun and hard work, demanding total concentration. My book was finally published two years ago, and now I am a proud author, even if I haven't made the best-seller list yet. In spite of the onslaught of illness, I realize how lucky I have been. In gratitude, I hope to live with courage, humility, and compassion.

Cleaning Lady - a treasured friend.

Chapter 5: The Staff

We just had our annual employee appreciation party, our only tangible way to thank the service staff. The residents' handbook stresses that we must not give direct tips or gifts, which might cause endless complications. Therefore, toward the end of the year, we anonymously give checks to an appreciation fund. This fund is divided by a special formula so that each service member receives a holiday check according to their work time. The checks (a goodly sum) are handed out at this party, as our resident council chairman offers our official thanks. In return, we receive many handshakes and hugs. The next day many thank-you cards are posted on a big lobby display.

Since there is more than one service person per resident, they carry out many different services, some seen and some not. The resident service attends to all resident activities, the administration service handles numerous daily operations of the place, the building service maintains the physical plant, the marketing service interviews and accepts new residents, the dining service feeds us daily, and the security service keeps us safe. We also have a housekeeping service to provide a cleaning woman once a week. A facility maintenance service does the plumbing, heating, electrical repairs, and other odd jobs. The security service does an important daily door check at each apartment. Every night a tiny tab over the jam of a closed door is tipped up. In the morning, it is checked to see if it has fallen, to show the door has been opened. If not, a staff member will phone, knock, or look in to be sure the resident is all right. Residents living alone who had strokes or falls have been found this way. All these services are included in the monthly fee.

The home health service offers many health activities at a reasonable fee. In emergencies nurses will come immediately to your apartment when summoned by phone or emergency pull cord (these cords are in every room) to check vital signs, and if the condition warrants, they will call an ambulance to take you to the hospital. In addition, if requested they will go to your apartment to dress wounds and give insulin or other injections. Residents may go to their office to check blood pressure anytime. Routine blood tests can be drawn there, especially for those on anticoagulants or those who are diabetics. They oversee nurses in the other healthcare units for the sicker and more disabled. Every fall we line up with arms bared so their nurses may give us influenza vaccine injections.

The physical therapy staff members provide an ongoing service for those needing instructions after surgery or for chronic nerve or joint disability. Availability of these health services makes it possible for many residents to remain in their apartments, which are a boon and a great relief.

As I look back, I realize running a house had been a great effort. To save the high price of plumbers, I would wait for two or three jobs before calling one. Ditto for electricians. Finding a good cleaning woman for a four-bedroom house was often difficult, so I had one come every two weeks and cleaned up myself during the week. Needless to say, the place was not always as neat as I would have liked. Although I like to cook, making lunch and supper day after day sometimes became tiresome. When it snowed John and I would be out shoveling the driveway. We went to the nearby medical center for routine medical care. When an acute episode occurred, such as a fainting spell, the spouse took the sick one to the emergency room. Security was our own responsibility. This meant locking our doors and not coming home in the dark at night. We managed, but not as well as we have done under the good care at Shangrila.

Katy, our cleaning woman, not only thoroughly cleans our apartment each week, but she is proactive. In her early thirties, she is tall, with a round pink face and blue eyes, and is mature beyond her years. She moves quickly to get much done in a short time. She created ways to get rid of mites on my food shelves. Twice a year she cleans out the refrigerator. After the terrorism scare, she rotated or tossed out any expired emergency food supplies. When she found my garbage disposal slowed up, she notified the facilities service to replace it. She scrubs my kitchen and dining room carpets, which are often soiled by spilled food. When vacuuming she maneuvers around John's many boxes on the floor. We often chat, and I've heard of the ups and downs in her busy life at home. Katy has become a treasured friend.

The facility maintenance staff members are always helpful. Besides fixing equipment that needed repairs, they helped us make the place safer to prevent more falls. They change our water filters about every six months. They have replaced our room thermometers twice, each time with a better one. They taught me how to plug equipment into the correct electrical wall sockets. They hung all our pictures. They helped us put up special wall shelves. We find them invaluable.

Seldom seen but essential is the security service. The entrance to Shangrila via the skyway is controlled by the resident's key card. When the card is inserted, a camera sees the person at the security office and at our main receptionist's desk. We are warned not to let unauthorized people follow us into the building. If they do, we notify the receptionist. She also carefully checks each visitor entering the front door before they are allowed in. We all have apartment keys and are told to lock our doors whenever we leave our apartments. Security guards patrol our corridors both day and night. In these days of increased crime, we really appreciate these extra precautions.

Our waitresses and waiters are young people, many in high school or college. They are trained by our dining room director to be courteous and efficient. The food arrives hot and in sequence. They are ready to replace any item we don't like. Halfway through the meal, they make sure all is to our satisfaction. During the holidays, they decorate the tables and are dressed in holiday clothes. We owe them thanks for making our dining such a pleasure.

The many service personnel are young or middle aged. Since there is a low turnover rate, we have come to know many of them. They are always courteous, helpful, and efficient. I cannot remember ever having a whole cadre of people devoted to making my life comfortable, pleasant, and safe. What a precious resource!

They must sometimes deal with irritable residents. These people wear a perpetual frown and never seem satisfied no matter what is done. Other residents don't want to be near them, which of course makes them even crabbier. However, I never heard a staff person reply with a cross word. I think they don't take the irritability personally, because they know it springs from deep wells of frustration and depression.

Two other facilities add immensely to our lives: the beauty parlor and the eatery. Most women go to a beauty parlor once a month for either a haircut or curl. However, after entering Shangrila, many become unable to wash their own hair, so in order to look nice, they make regular weekly appointments. This service is a great morale booster. Ann, the beauty parlor owner, is a no-nonsense brown-haired woman of about forty-five who seems to know what every woman resident needs. She suggests different hairdos so that long hair gives way to shorter hair and curled hair gives way to simpler straight hair. This happened to me after my operations. A good businesswoman, she doubled the size of the beauty parlor to accommodate more of us. I hope she continues to do well financially, as we need her very much, not only for her skill but also for her unique understanding.

The eatery was installed about three years ago. It is four times as big as the previous smaller room that only sold hot soup and sandwiches and a few necessities. Half the enlarged space is a restaurant with small tables where people can eat and chat. A menu of hot foods is also now available. The other half is a store selling milk, orange juice, soft drinks, sandwiches, many kinds of canned and dry goods, as well as cards, jewelry, ornaments, and toys. Never empty, it has become a popular place where residents as well as employees gather to talk and eat small meals throughout the day. We all pick up convenient things in the store. This is a real Shangrila asset.

Books! Books! More under the Christmas tree.

Chapter 6: The Reality

On weekdays, I awake around 7:00 a.m. and step into the kitchen to make breakfast, then walk next door to eat it with my husband. It's all close and convenient. He goes down to the lobby floor for the newspaper and often buys orange juice and milk at the eatery. We avidly read the newspaper. About 9:00 or 10:00 a.m., I teach my tai chi class or participate in a scheduled exercise class to keep me looking good and feeling good. For the rest of the morning, John works next door at his computer, and I handle the mail or to-do jobs. Sometimes I cross the skyway to go to the bank or buy items at the nearby subway drugstore.

At noon, I make a quick lunch of soup, sandwich, or salad. In the afternoon, John may take the car on errands while I attend an in-house talk or concert. Once a fortnight we drive to the supermarket and load up on necessities and groceries for my simple meals. Alternatively, we may both go in the van on a half-day trip to a nearby city museum or event, or in summer we may go for a Mississippi River cruise.

The cleaning lady will have been by when we return to a clean tidy apartment. In the background the facilities staff will have kept our windows clean, our heating and cooling systems working, and even our fire alarm sensors in top condition.

For supper we usually enjoy an ethnic-cuisine buffet or we arrange a take-out meal so we can watch TV as we eat. Once a week, I indulge in cooking dinner, or we go out to eat. The evening TV news is a must to keep up on the stock market, politics, and world news. We may then attend an evening concert or talk downstairs. Otherwise, we read the latest books or work at the computer. Bedtime is around 10:00 p.m. for me, later for John. We have had a productive and pleasant day and will awake to a new day.

Sundays are a little different. In the mornings, we watch the summary of the week's TV news, and then go to a delicious Sunday buffet where we are often joined by invited outside friends. Afternoons are spent reading or going for a walk, outdoors if the weather is nice, indoors if it is nasty. When it snows, I say to myself, "Thank God, we don't have to shovel." Around 4:00 p.m. I attend vespers at our chapel, where I enjoy singing my favorite hymns and thinking spiritual thoughts. Supper is very simple. Around seven thirty, we often see an old classic movie downstairs. Then it's more reading and working at the computer before bed. With a happy sigh, we look forward to next week.

The advantage of a gadget–loving spouse is that we have Tivo to record special TV shows and play them back whenever we wish, a copy machine to copy documents or news articles to share with others, and a shredder to destroy discarded documents. He has a new cell phone on which I can contact him anytime he is out of the apartment.

∾

Each day we exchange pleasantries with numerous residents we meet in corridors, elevators, at meals, or at events. I know that whenever I feel sick we can pull the emergency cord for the health care service or contact our doctor at the nearby medical facility. During this time of life, John and I can think of no other place we would rather be than in this happy community that is so comfortable, convenient, and safe.

While we live in a sheltered world, we cannot totally escape the real world. Y2K catapulted John and me into Shangrila. A few of us know soldiers now serving in Afghanistan and Iraq. One resident's daughter was caught in the Hurricane Katrina flood; another had her Florida home partially destroyed by water. We exercise our precious voting rights at the polls for local and national elections. We often have public affairs meetings to discuss ongoing events. We also have speakers who suggest emergency measures in case of an avian flu outbreak or terrorism attack. Homeland security impacts us when we wait in long lines at airports, to be searched before boarding.

Our city is probably not important enough to be a terrorist target, but casualties will probably pour into our regional trauma center from surrounding areas. We at Shangrila have our own plans for care and protection of occupants. The many retired physicians and nurses living here will be a definite asset.

Meanwhile, we must get on with day-to-day living. I saw an article entitled "Do you have enough for your retirement?" Good question. Many of us have lived longer than we anticipated, and prices rise yearly. How will we pay for these years? Soon-to-retire Baby Boomers better start saving right away if they have not already. The only trick I know is to have an investment strategy to stay ahead of inflation and increasing medical expenses. A wise Shangrila friend told me she put her entire estate in the hands of a highly reputable money-managing firm years ago. They do all the work (for a fee) and she simply glances at yearly reports. By this means, she has been able to go all over the world (including such places as Mongolia and Antarctica) without a care about expenses and still have enough for the rest of her life. Many would like to be in her shoes.

I started investing during my working years, and even more assiduously in retirement. I've marched along first with stocks, then with bonds, then mutual funds, and now exchange-traded funds. I have stayed ahead of inflation and made some money. This activity keeps me eagerly reading papers and listening to national and international business and political news. I heartily recommend this endeavor.

Books! Books! Books! My dear spouse is a bookaholic! Every week we get one or two new books from Amazon. com or the local bookstore. We have the latest computer books, history books, economy books, how-to books, and books on politics, music, and even religion. Every time John hears about a good book, I can wager it will arrive in a few days. He doesn't buy fiction, because he believes real world-events are far more fascinating and worth knowing about. I believe he has a point. I confess I also add to our book-buying and read many of the purchased books. If I want to read fiction, I go to our little library. For John's purposes borrowing from the public library doesn't work, since they seldom have recently published technical books, and we like to underline as we read.

He loves a hilarious new book, *The Perfect Mess*, because it justifies his messiness. If we must have an extravagance, this is as good as any. It keeps us attuned to the world and gives us immeasurable pleasure. However, our apartment overflows with books! At the end of the year, he sorts out ones to discard and packs them in boxes to donate to libraries, schools, or to our sidewalk sale. We can hardly keep up. I have further added to the problem, for I am now in the exciting throes of writing another book.

I am a part of Shangrila now. It is my home. I am, oh so happy here. It has been six years since we moved here. Christmas is again upon us with all its wonder and beauty. Shangrila is full of Christmas activities. The Christmas buffet menu is mouth-watering. Christmas trees, holly wreaths, and poinsettias are everywhere. Carols ring in the halls. Everyone is going around with cards and gifts.

My greatest wish is for "peace on earth, goodwill to men."